RELEASING THE LIGHT

Water Lilies at Dawn

In the first light of dawn, while everything is still damp
and motionless, the delicate lily petals unfold
slowly to glow in the morning sun.

Watercolour, 28" x 7", 1996; published
as a limited edition in 1996

RELEASING THE LIGHT

The Art of
Carol Evans

RAINCOAST BOOKS

Vancouver

To Bryn, whose vision and gentle wisdom help
me to recognize what I value most

First published in 1997 by
Raincoast Books
8680 Cambie Street
Vancouver, B.C.
V6P 6M9
(604) 323-7100

CANADIAN CATALOGUING IN PUBLICATION DATA

Evans, Carol.
Releasing the light

ISBN 1-55192-074-3 (bound) — ISBN 1-55192-067-0 (pbk.)

1. Evans, Carol. 2. Pacific Coast (B.C.) in art. I. Title.
ND1843.E92A4 1997   759.11   C96-910696-3

To order the collector's edition or autographed hardcover copies of this book,
or for information regarding limited-edition prints, please contact:

Dayspring Studio, Inc.
P.O. Box #94, Fulford Harbour
Salt Spring Island, B.C.
Canada V8K 2P2
Phone: (250) 653-4479   Fax: (250) 653-4170
Toll Free: (800) 667-2366

Designed by Dean Allen
Project Editor: Michael Carroll
Copy Editor: Rachelle Kanefsky

Printed and bound in Hong Kong

Raincoast Books gratefully acknowledges the support of the Canada Council, the
Department of Canadian Heritage, and the British Columbia Arts Council.

Many thanks to Ken Budd, Joyce McLean, Bryn King, my family,
and all the capable people at Raincoast Books who helped to
produce this book, and especially to the
galleries who carry my work.

Tanya
A flood of sunlight creates a halo
around a small, tousled head.

Watercolour, 12 ½" x 19", 1985;
published as a limited edition in 1995

INTRODUCTION

I CREATED THESE PAINTINGS FOR YOU, for your eyes. My paintings are my memories, but more than that, they are my best attempt to show you some of the inspiration I find in nature – beauty that is seemingly simple and common, yet exquisite and perfect.

I believe there is an age-old door within our subconscious – at least within mine. It tends to feel like heavy hardwood, dark and solid, well built by distant ancestors. On one side of it is the frenetic complexity of everyday life. On the other, is a quiet wilderness that is timeless, eternal, and simple, with sunlight, moonlight, the seasons, and the smaller things – twigs, leaves, flower petals. Although the door opens easily outward, it can seem so difficult to find time away from the inevitable routines of life to enter nature's quiet refuge. Yet for me – and I would venture to guess for many – there is a sense of yearning, a sense of calling.

In my life, it is light that beckons the strongest. Sometimes it happens unexpectedly. In the midst of a busy morning, a bright beam of sunlight will pour through the kitchen window, glint off the toaster, and stream across the floor, filling the entire room with golden light until I simply can't ignore it. I stop, perhaps for only a moment, to enjoy its warm radiance before getting back to the work at hand. There are times when that is all we can do, stop for a moment and notice. But how wonderful it is to follow that beckoning. I have discovered profound benefits in stopping the clock and ignoring chores to walk through my door into wilderness, into the expansive outdoor world, eyes squinting in sunlight.

I see this book as a door, swinging out invitingly into bright sun, a steady breeze, cedars, moss, salal, the beach, and assorted flotsam and jetsam. Most of my paintings

Daffodils
*Bold, bright, freshly
picked daffodils.*

Watercolour, 13" x 9", 1988

1

are of places in and around that world; that lively, invigorating, refreshing, beguiling world of the Pacific coast. They are my efforts to express the sense of joy and exhilaration I feel in forests and around harbours. They are a celebration of this magnificent land.

The first impression is always sunlight, the primary concern of everything I paint. No matter what the subject, my process of painting is entirely influenced by light: its direction, the shadows it creates, its honey glow causing everything to hover on a cushion of warm air. Light penetrates things, revealing inner qualities and colours, like the veins in a leaf or the translucence of a shell. It creates halos around them. It makes things shine and flash and reach out to you, come alive. It rings out like sound echoing here and there off everything, filling a place with its reflected glow like a visual symphony. It has a divine loveliness to it. It appears without any human hand causing it to appear. It is just there, and a scene is blessed with its rays. My work is to reflect it in my painting.

I am endlessly fascinated with trying to depict light and all its million facets. It sparks my imagination, and I revel in the challenge of trying to pull it out, to release it. More than anything else, my decision to paint a scene is based on an engaging light. A place can look muted and flat, or vibrant and alive, depending on the light. While a beach may be interesting, full of impressive colours and shapes, if the lighting is dull, it doesn't occur to me to paint it. But when the sun highlights a scene – and it may be a fairly ordinary scene – it catches my attention. A common sight, even a relatively mundane setting, will become illuminated. It practically sings with radiance, and everything becomes extraordinary. Then it is not the artist capturing the scene, but the scene capturing the artist. It is an uplifting moment, one when a new painting is born. It is not just the scene itself that comes to life, but how the sunlight plays within the scene.

Beyond the bright light of a summer day, there is a broad spectrum of other kinds of light, each with its own inherent mood. There is the luminous half-light of dawn with its haunting, hidden presence. There is light diffused by cloud or haze, layered in mist that veils trees and islands, transforming them into ghostlike forms. There is dim twilight borrowed from a setting sun – a faint, warm blush like a fading memory. And finally, the pale wash of mystic moonlight. So often there is incredible beauty in changing light. It is not as dramatic, perhaps, as dancing sunlight, but

Sunlit Rose

Even the innermost petals of a
yellow rose are aglow in the sun.

Watercolour, 10" x 13", 1988

a subtler, quieter, darker beauty. This mysterious, softer light is critical to setting a mood or inspiring a moment of quiet reflection, and is equally compelling as the heat and brightness of a noonday sun.

Another inspirational influence, as well as the light, is this land that meanders and jogs along the edge of the ocean. Where the elemental forces of earth and water interact, forming miles and miles of bluffs and bays and beaches, there is an irresistible visual feast of reflections, movements, and textures – and the vast horizon. I am in awe of the beauty created by the unseen hand of the elements: massive sandstone cliffs sculpted by the wind, gnarled sun-bleached logs, a ribbon of seaweed delicately placed across a porcelain shell by the retreating tide. These are the signs and traces of the forces of nature: the sun, the rain, the tides, and the chiselling wind. Many of my paintings are portrayals of their artistry.

When I slog through salal bushes or wander along a beach and see some evocative image, maybe a collection of stones or shells, the vision awakens the artist in me and transforms the image into inspiration. I see in my mind's eye how it would look as a painting. The rest of the work is pulling together my tools and abilities to get the vision out, to distil its essence onto paper.

Watercolour paint is a natural medium for me. It complements and enhances the beauty of this coastal panorama. This region is, after all, a damp, misty part of the world a lot of the time. Water hangs in great silken sheets of fog across mountains and inlets. It ripples and reflects along the shore. The wet, delicate, and raw subtleties of watercolour washes are ideal for conveying the gradation of light within clouds or a summer haze, perfect for suggesting shapes and forms barely visible in shrouded mist or streaking rain. It has a characteristic fresh, organic quality that easily gives the impression of trees and plants, and of rock formations and their textures. It is quick and spontaneous, and has a simplicity to it, requiring few tools – *and* it cannot quite be tamed!

I am unashamedly infatuated with watercolour as a medium. In truth, it is my silent partner. It plays a role that I could not possibly play myself. It does things I cannot control and creates effects that no human hand could repeat. Each wet wash has limitless potential for a brief, exciting period of time. Once I unleash the colours into the water, they go to work flowing, spreading, fanning out, and merging until they finally settle into a vibrant, natural bloom . . . and then dry.

During that process, I can only stand by and watch, drink tea, and wait. I have learned from experience that I have to leave a wash alone, untouched and free. If it ends up darker than I intended – perhaps making an island appear closer – so be it. I let it have its own life. If I trifle with it, I lose that bloom of freshness. How true is fellow artist Robert Amos's observation that watercolour washes are equal parts intention, chemistry, and divine intervention.

In my work, there is always tension between freedom and control. While I want a painting to have spontaneity, I also want my subject to be recognizable. I take the time to plan the painting and draw it out. Using masking fluid, I mask out the light areas and concentrate on painting the focal point, the area that is the central focus in the scene. I still apply washes, but they are smaller and more controlled.

I am a developing artist, always learning and experimenting, but I would describe my current painting style as a marriage between loose, "washy" areas, blended with tighter, representational painting. I think of my paintings as portraits, mirroring specific places or subjects in my surroundings. So when a beach inspires me, I search out ways to convey its unique character, just as I might do when painting a portrait of a person. I look for the most complimentary view and the essence or the spark of life within the subject. In the end, when the painting is finished, it is my hope that it reveals something of the likeness of the place in its best light, at its finest moment.

Nothing gives me more pleasure than when someone recognizes a beach in my painting and remembers, "sitting on that rock right there!" So often that person has a special relationship to the beach, a personal connection. We probably all have places where we feel good and where we are uplifted. I have several special spots that have seen me through a lot of changes, where I can sit and soak up the sweetness of reflection. I believe we gain more strength and derive more sustenance from being outside than we can possibly know. The benefits are immeasurable, yet we are mostly unaware of exactly what they are and how deeply they affect us.

Nature's rugged domain has an all-embracing power and grace that is so very quiet, simple, and unobtrusive. That is why I am preoccupied with trying to capture it in my work. Of course, I never do, because it is too fleeting and too elusive. There is something in the rocks and the trees and the clouds, something more than meets the eye. Maybe something to be learned. But it is not discernible within our conscious thoughts. I think it is more a thing to be felt, permeating our being over time.

All I know is that I feel fully alive when I spend time in the natural world. I feel whole. I am reassured, comforted, soothed. Outside in the wind, with the smell of the trees, next to the sea, with silky sand slipping through my fingers, I am enchanted, reawakened, and reconnected to our Maker.

Painting is not a technical skill for me. It is a way of communicating, and the light I am studying is a direction. All living things position themselves to face the light and to grow toward it, and our own existence is arranged around it. When I paint this beautiful land, I am painting Someone else's artistry. What I am attempting to record is the life force that is in every creation.

When I see beautiful, natural light streaming across a beach, flooding a mountain slope, or dappling a moss carpet, I am stirred, and I yearn, through my painting, to release the brilliance of that light for my eyes – and for yours.

Sunset over Vesuvius Bay
A moment of glory before the tangerine light of the sun slips behind the hills.

Watercolour, 12" x 19", 1985

Seabright Garden

A colourful burst of spring flowers
graces vegetable boxes at the
edge of the sea.

Watercolour, 18" x 13 ¼", 1995

With the presence of light, an

event is transformed and

its essential beauty

is revealed.

Sally and Shawna
Sun-bright curls and happy faces
in the early-morning light.

Watercolour, 14¼" x 11½", 1986;
chosen for a Christmas card by
Amnesty International, 1986

When we are introduced to the

outdoors, we are introduced to

an old and faithful

lifelong friend.

Fishermen at Fernwood
*In the vibrant reflection of the evening
sun, a father and his boy set
out to do a little fishing.*

Watercolour, 19" x 26", 1985

Floating Flowers
Sunshine accentuates pure delight
reflected in the girls' faces.

Watercolour, 12 ¾" x 16 ¾", 1992;
published as a limited edition in 1993

Mesmerized by the Sea

The intensity of the girls' concentration is eclipsed only by the sudden burst of sunlight in their bucket.

Watercolour, 17" x 28", 1995

"To see a world in a grain of sand

And a heaven in a wild flower,

Hold infinity in the palm of your hand

And eternity in an hour."

— WILLIAM BLAKE, *Auguries of Innocence*

Life at the Edge of the Sea

Dwarfed by the grandness of the setting, in a scene suffused by
summer light, two girls focus their attention on
the edge of a wave and the treasures
brought forth from the sea.

Watercolour, 28" x 20¼", 1995;
winner of the People's Choice Award at the
Nature of Island Artists Exhibition,
Gold Stream Park, B.C., in 1995

Coastal Home

An eagle glides soundlessly past a streak of wood smoke,
which blends into fog at the shoreline.

Watercolour, 13 ¼" x 19 ½", 1990

Sheltered Cove

Queen Ann's Lace and sea grasses grow in profusion at the edge of a quiet cove.

Watercolour, 20 ⅛" x 27 ⅞", 1993

Wilderness reflects the beauty, the

mystery, of its Creator and carries

healing in its wings.

Headlands

Mirrored in still water, gulls
gaze at a rolling sea.

Watercolour, 19" x 12½", 1994

Maybe it is the clarity,

reflection, movement, and depth,

but there is something even beyond

words that makes water

so hypnotic.

Deep Pool

A collection of sea anemones delicately open
and close in a clear, sunlit pool.

Watercolour, 20 ¼" x 12 ⅞", 1995

Light and Shadow on Shell Beach

*There is a wonderful interplay between warm, bright sunlight
and cool, turquoise shadows across a
backdrop of white shells.*

Watercolour, 12 ½" x 19", 1985;
published as a companion print to
the collector's edition of this book in 1997

Low Tide

*Only a clear pool of seawater remains after the
tide withdraws, reflecting the grey sky
across its serene surface.*

Watercolour, 25 ⅛" x 42 ⅛", 1993

Sunlight Captured by the Sea

Slanting rays of sun create a profusion of light in rolling waves that break on rock, and the muted colours of an evening sea explode into radiance.

Watercolour, 12⅞" x 20⅜", 1994;
published as a limited edition in 1995

Mystic Beach

*A wave hurls itself at sandstone bluffs, bursting into spray
and foam, only to be followed by another
and yet another . . .*

Watercolour, 23 ¾" x 42 ¾", 1994

Cusheon Lake

Clear, tea-coloured water appears as an
invitation on a hot summer day.

Watercolour, 12⅞" x 20⅜", 1994

Lily and the Frog

*With attention drawn to the sunny, pink petals of a
water lily, it is easy to overlook a
motionless frog nearby.*

Watercolour, 13" x 19", 1988

Past all obstacles and barriers, water

inevitably finds its way.

Chatterbox Falls

*A thundering sheet of water cascades down, pounding onto rocks
and exploding into spray, then re-forms into a
burbling stream and courses to the sea.*

Watercolour, 20¼" x 12¾", 1993;
published as a limited edition in 1994

Swim out into the lake and the

whole world disappears but for

small dancing ripples and

whispering reeds.

The Swimmer

The calm water of the lake, reflecting dark trees
surrounding it, bursts into light with
every movement of the swimmer.

Watercolour, 19 ⅛" x 28", 1995;
published as a limited edition in 1995

Big Qualicum River Crossing

Its shadow cast onto clear waters below, the train,
in turn, reflects the sky above.

Watercolour, 28 ¼" x 20", 1988;
published as a limited edition in 1988

Light and Sea

Triangles of light emblazoned by the sun
move across a blue sea backdrop.

Watercolour, 28 ¾" x 19 ¼", 1996

It is a blessing beyond measure

to live near the sea.

Fulford Morning
Swans grace the sparkling waters of a
low tide in Fulford Harbour.

Watercolour, 20¼" x 12⅞", 1995

Morning in Active Pass

*An eastbound tug plows through the waters of Active
Pass in the warm morning light.*

Watercolour, 6" x 18", 1996;
published as a limited edition in 1997

Early Run / Active Pass

*While water dances and seagulls weave and circle in the pink
morning light, a tug on an early run pushes purposefully
through the tide surge.*

Watercolour, 6 ⅛" x 15 ⅛", 1996;
published as a limited edition in 1997

Flight in Sunlight

*With sun caught in gulls' wings, the scene becomes a
play of reflecting and moving light.*

Watercolour, 20 ⅛" x 28", 1993;
published as a limited edition in 1994

Mist has a way of slowly, imperceptibly,

moving to reveal entire landscapes

previously hidden. Things

come into view as if

out of nowhere.

Call Above the River
A shrill call pierces the leaden sky.

Watercolour, 24 ¾" x 20 ⅛", 1990

Turning of the Tide
Late-afternoon sun floods the channel as a rising tide rushes between the islands.

Watercolour, 24" x 42", 1996

Touched by the sun, every

insignificant twig and filament

becomes a pathway of light.

Spring Robins
Early spring sun illuminates a tangle of
branches and flitting wings.

Watercolour, 19 ¾" x 13 ⅛", 1990

Swans in Fulford Harbour
*With necks gracefully curved, swans gleam
in the morning sun.*

Watercolour, 19" x 26", 1987

Feeding the Swans

Reaching toward the girl's outstretched hand,
dazzling white swans on shining water
appear as light upon light.

Watercolour, 19 ½" x 39 ⅜", 1996

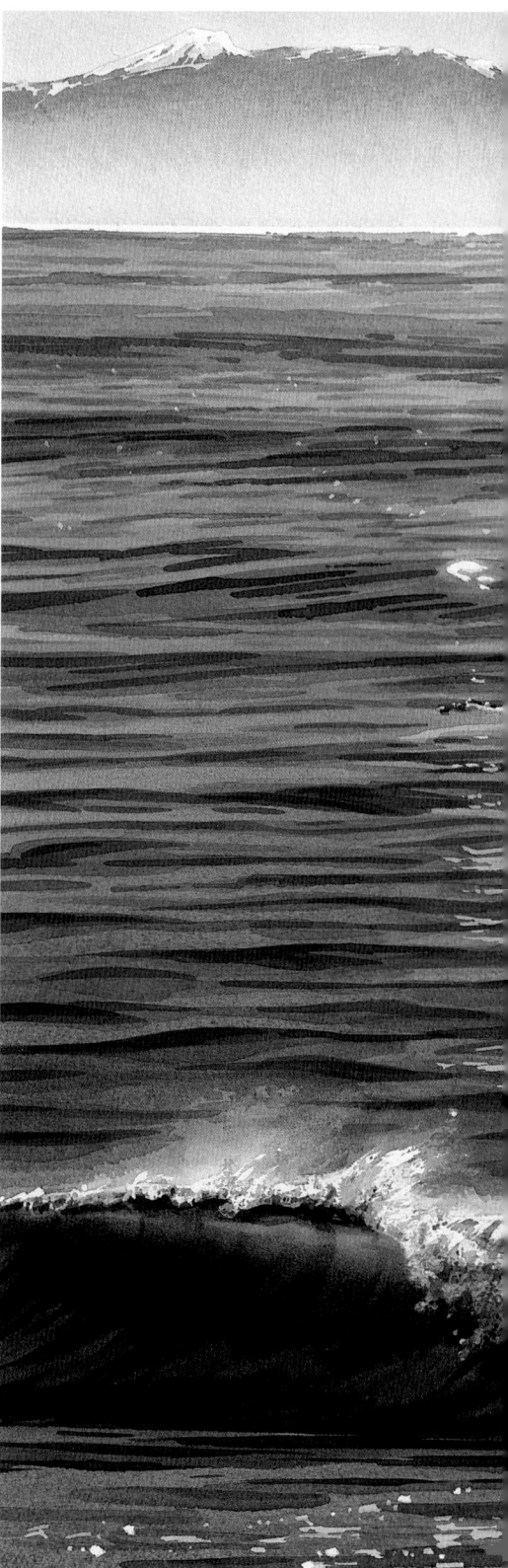

Gulls on a Log

*Stationed on a drifting log, gulls become
part of an undulating sea.*

Watercolour, 20 ¼" x 27 ⅝", 1994;
published as a limited edition in 1994

Fishing Tree

Eagles await the moment of opportunity.

Watercolour, 27" x 13 ½", 1995

Evening Sky, Reflected
Wet sand reflects evening colours so faithfully,
one could imagine running
across the sky in bare feet.

Watercolour, 30 ⅜" x 13 ⅜", 1996

How quickly the sun enters a

scene and reveals beauty in many

layers. And how quickly

it moves on again.

Rose on a Glass Table

Sunlight illuminates a Fragrant Cloud rose resplendent
among stones and sweet grass on a collection of shells.

Watercolour, 18" x 12¾", 1995

Flowers of One Garden

A shimmering display of wildflowers in an
untamed mountain garden.

Watercolour, 28" x 20", 1991;
published as a limited edition in 1992

Canoe

Bearing the artistry of a tradition centuries old, a newly made canoe sits at the water's edge.

Watercolour, 12 ½" x 19", 1986

Ninstints

*Weatherworn poles cast shadows across the ground but
share little of the stories they could tell.*

Watercolour, 26" x 19", 1987

Sea of Light, Shore of Mystery

*There was a time when a thriving village spilled
outward from the poles. In the afternoons — then, as
now — the western sun danced over the trees and
onto the water but left the village in shadow.*

Watercolour, 28" x 20 ¼", 1993;
published as a limited edition in 1993

Migrating South

A small pod of orcas pass Thormanby Island on their
way down the Strait of Georgia.

Watercolour, 13" x 19½", 1995;
published as a limited edition in 1996

Dawn Breakers

Their calls breaking the silence,
ravens rush across a dawn sky.

Watercolour, 20" x 27 ⅝", 1994

Sea Lions at Sunset

*Luxuriating in warm sun, sea lions languish
on a rock outcropping.*

Watercolour, 12 ⅞" x 20 ⅛", 1993

"Let what we love be what we do.

There are hundreds of ways to kneel

and kiss the ground."

— JELALUDDIN RUMI

Moshe

No matter how many things clutter the windowsill, Moshe
finds a place to sit and gaze out at
nothing in particular.

Watercolour, 21 ½" x 13", 1995;
published as a limited edition in 1996